DISCOVERING THE UNITED STATES

Rhode Island

BY JANET SLINGERLAND

Kids Core
An Imprint of Abdo Publishing
abdobooks.com

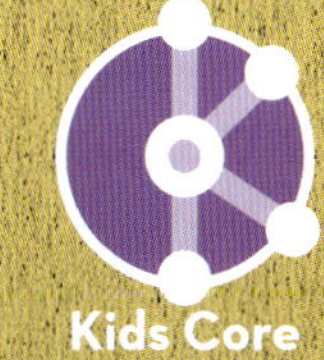

abdobooks.com

Printed in China.
052024
092024

Cover Photos: iStockphoto (background); Dana Bibeault/Shutterstock Images (boats)
Interior Photos: North Wind Picture Archives/Alamy, 4–5; Darryl Brooks/Shutterstock Images, 7; Marilyn Barbone/Shutterstock Images, 8 (top left); iStockphoto, 8 (top right); Shutterstock Images, 8 (bottom left), 10; Beth Fitzpatrick/Shutterstock Images, 8 (bottom right); Sean D. Elliot/The Day/AP Images, 12–13; Ivy Close Images/Alamy, 14; Abel Uribe/Chicago Tribune/TNS/McClatchy-Tribune/Tribune Content Agency LLC/Alamy Live News/Alamy, 17; Kristoffer Tripplaar/Alamy, 18; Wangkun Jia/Shutterstock Images, 20–21; Douglas Mason/Getty Images Entertainment/Getty Images, 23; LnP Images/Shutterstock Images, 25; Michael Sean O'Leary/Shutterstock Images, 26; Red Line Editorial, 28 (map), 29; EWY Media/Shutterstock Images, 28 (Tennis Hall of Fame); James Kirkikis/Shutterstock Images, 28 (Slater Mill)

Editor: Haley Williams
Series Designer: Katharine Hale

Library of Congress Control Number: 2023949550

Publisher's Cataloging-in-Publication Data

Names: Slingerland, Janet, author.
Title: Rhode Island / by Janet Slingerland
Description: Minneapolis, Minnesota: Abdo Publishing, 2025 | Series: Discovering the United States | Includes online resources and index.
Identifiers: ISBN 9781098294106 (lib. bdg.) | ISBN 9798384913375 (ebook)
Subjects: LCSH: U.S. states--Juvenile literature. | Rhode Island--History--Juvenile literature. | Northeastern States--Juvenile literature. | Physical geography--United States--Juvenile literature.
Classification: DDC 973--dc23

All population data taken from:
"Estimates of Population by Sex, Race, and Hispanic Origin: April 1, 2020 to July 1, 2022." *US Census Bureau, Population Division*, June 2023, census.gov.

CONTENTS

Today, the area where the HMS *Gaspee* got stuck is known as Gaspee Point.

CHAPTER 1

The Gaspee Affair

It was June 9, 1772. A British ship called the HMS *Gaspee* was chasing a small ship around Rhode Island waters. The British were hoping to catch **smugglers**. But the *Gaspee* got stuck near the shores of the town of Warwick.

American **colonists** saw this as an opportunity. They wanted to attack the ship to stop British control in the area. Shortly after midnight, the colonists surrounded the *Gaspee* in small boats. They boarded the ship and captured the crew. Then, the colonists burned down the *Gaspee*.

Today, this event is known as the Gaspee Affair. Historians believe it helped spark the American Revolutionary War (1775–1783). The Gaspee Affair continues to be an important part of Rhode Island's history.

Land

Rhode Island sits in the Northeast region of the United States. It is the smallest US state.

People enjoy sailing on the many bodies of water in Rhode Island.

Connecticut borders Rhode Island to the west. Massachusetts lies to the east and north. And the Atlantic Ocean is to the south.

There are also many islands that make up Rhode Island. The largest of these is Block Island.

Rhode Island Facts

DATE OF STATEHOOD
May 29, 1790

CAPITAL
Providence

POPULATION
1,093,734

AREA
1,545 square miles
(4,002 sq km)

STATE BIRD

Rhode Island Red chicken

STATE TREE

Red maple

STATE FLOWER

Violet

STATE SHELL

Quahog

Each US state has a different population, size, and capital city. States also have state symbols.

Block Island is about 10 miles (16 km) south from the state's coast. Rhode Island also has many bodies of water. This includes **inlets**, bays, and rivers. Rhode Island has about

400 miles (640 km) of coastline. Sandy beaches can be found along the coast.

About 60 percent of Rhode Island is covered by forests. Oak trees, white pines, and red maples can be found in many of the forests. Marshy lowlands surround the bay. The western part of the state is hilly.

Rhode Island Wildlife

Rhode Island has a variety of wildlife. Coyotes, raccoons, and skunks are common there. More than 400 different birds live in or visit Rhode Island. People can find ocean animals such as harbor seals and clams along the coast.

Rhode Island's flag features the state motto, "Hope." The flag also has a golden anchor, which is the state's coat of arms.

Climate

Rhode Island has cold winters and warm summers. The southwestern area is the coolest part of the state. Northern Rhode Island is usually the hottest. Temperatures can be more than 90 degrees Fahrenheit (32°C) for a few weeks during the summer.

Rhode Island experiences strong storms called nor'easters. Winds from these storms usually come from the northeast. Nor'easters bring heavy rain or snow, strong winds, and coastal flooding. They are most common between September and April. They often cause blizzards.

Further Evidence

Look at the website below. Does it give any new evidence to support Chapter One?

Rhode Island

abdocorelibrary.com/discovering-rhode-island

Many American Indian peoples in Rhode Island today still perform traditional dances, including the Eastern Blanket Dance.

The People of Rhode Island

The first American Indians lived in what is now Rhode Island more than 30,000 years ago. One of the first tribes was the Narragansett. They lived on the coast in the summer. In the winter, they moved inland. They often hunted, fished, and farmed.

In 1636, Roger Williams, *right*, established the first white settlement in Rhode Island. He got the land from the Narragansett people.

Today, the Narragansett Indian Tribe is the only federally recognized tribe in Rhode Island. Some other American Indian peoples in the state include the Wampanoag and the Pequot.

European **settlers** first arrived in Rhode Island in the 1600s. Most of these settlers were from England. In the 1800s, **immigrants** began arriving in Rhode Island. They included people from Ireland, Canada, Portugal, and southern Italy.

In 2022, about 1.1 million people lived in Rhode Island. Almost 70 percent of people were white. Hispanic or Latino people made up 18 percent of the population. About 9 percent of people were Black, and 4 percent were Asian.

Culture

Many of Rhode Island's popular dishes come from the sea. Stuffies are stuffed quahog clams. Clam meat is mixed with several ingredients.

This includes breadcrumbs, celery, and onions. The stuffing is loaded into half a clam shell. The clam is then baked.

Art is a big part of Rhode Island culture. The state has several well-known art and design schools. People can see others' work or show off their art at festivals or outdoor art exhibits. They can also visit museums and art galleries throughout the state.

Rhode Island Dishes

Rhode Island is known for several popular foods and drinks. Coffee milk is the state drink. Sweet coffee syrup is stirred into cold milk. Some people even add ice cream to it. Johnnycakes are a well-known Rhode Island food. They are cornmeal pancakes often eaten for breakfast.

The company Autocrat produces a coffee syrup that is often used to make coffee milk.

Industries

Rhode Islanders work in many different industries. Health care is a big industry in the state. Those in this industry may do research to help create better medical technology. Other people have jobs in hotels or food service.

The toy and game company Hasbro was founded in Providence in 1923. Today, the company's headquarters are based in Pawtucket.

Manufacturing is another top industry in the state. Rhode Island factories manufacture a lot of jewelry and metal goods.

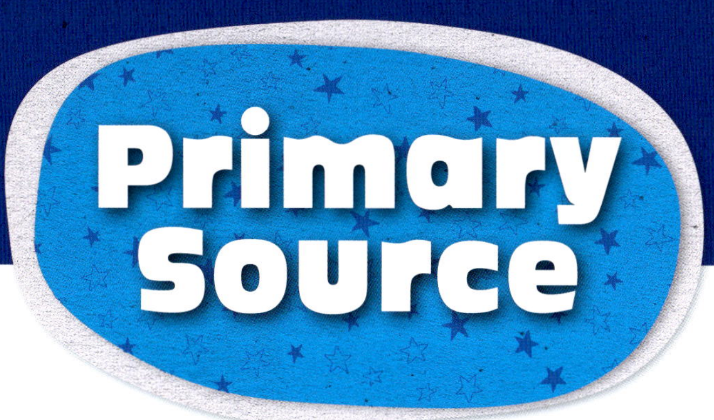

The Narragansett Indian Tribe's official website describes the summer and winter homes of its **ancestors**:

> The winter home [was] called a long house in which up to 20 families would live. . . . During the summer, the tribe would move to the shore and [build] . . . temporary shelter made of bark on the outside.

Source: "Early History," *Narragansett Indian Tribe*, n.d., narragansettindiannation.org. Accessed 12 Oct. 2023.

Comparing Texts

Think about the quote. Does it support the information in this chapter? Explain how in a few sentences.

The Newport Cliff Walk is a 3.5-mile (5.6-km) trail along Rhode Island's coast. It features historic mansions and beautiful ocean views.

CHAPTER 3

Places in Rhode Island

Providence is the capital of Rhode Island. It also has more people than any other city in the state. The city sits on the Providence River. Providence has become well known for its great food and art. Newport is another big city in Rhode Island.

Many tourists go there to see the huge mansions the city is known for.

Parks

There are several parks in Rhode Island. Blackstone River Valley National Historical Park is in the eastern part of the state. Slater Mill is a building in the park that historians believe is where the American Industrial Revolution began. This was a period in the late 1800s when a lot of new technology was created. Today, people can visit Slater Mill. They can also go biking, hiking, or canoeing in the park.

Fort Adams State Park sits on Newport Harbor. The fort in the park was used by the US Army and then the US Navy until 1965.

The Newport Jazz Festival has been held at Fort Adams State Park since 1981.

Today, the park hosts jazz and folk music festivals. It also offers great views of the surrounding water in the area.

Landmarks

Rhode Island has many beautiful landmarks. The state is home to five National Wildlife **Refuges**. Most of the refuges are along the coast. One is on Block Island. These wildlife refuges are important for migratory birds.

The Washington–Rochambeau Revolutionary Route cuts through parts of Rhode Island. This trail goes from Virginia to Massachusetts. It runs through the cities of Providence and Newport. The trail honors the joining of French and American soldiers during the American Revolutionary War. Visitors can see a historic Rhode Island farm and fort along the route.

International Tennis Hall of Fame

The International Tennis Hall of Fame is located in Newport. It was founded in 1954. The museum honors the history of tennis. Visitors can learn more about the important people and moments throughout tennis history. They can also play tennis on one of the many courts there.

The Arcade Providence is the oldest indoor shopping mall in the United States. The mall was built in 1828.

One of the nation's oldest carousels is found in Rhode Island. The Flying Horse Carousel sits on the southwestern coast. The carousel was built in 1876. It first traveled with a circus. It has been in the town of Westerly since 1897.

Although people cannot go into the tower of the North Light Lighthouse, they can visit the museum there.

Rhode Island also has several famous lighthouses. Some are still used by the US Coast Guard. Block Island has two lighthouses. The North Light was built in 1868. The Southeast Light was built in 1875. People can go to the island and visit both lighthouses.

Rhode Island is the smallest US state. But it has a lot to offer. People can visit its many historical sites. They can try some of the state's popular dishes. Or they can have fun in its cities and towns. Rhode Island has something for everyone.

Explore Online

Visit the website below. What new information did you learn that wasn't in Chapter Three?

Blackstone River Valley National Historical Park

abdocorelibrary.com/discovering-rhode-island

State Map

KEY

 Capital
 City or town
 Point of interest

Park

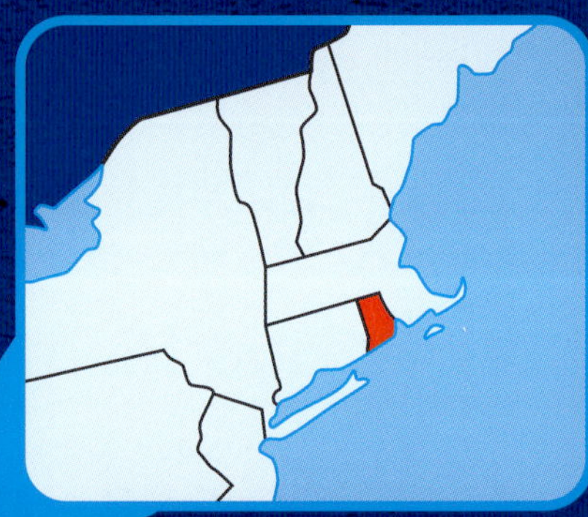

International Tennis Hall of Fame

Slater Mill

Rhode Island: The Ocean State

Glossary

ancestors
the people from whom a person is descended and who lived many generations ago

colonists
people who live in an area controlled by another country

immigrants
people who move to a different country

inlets
narrow waterways that run between two pieces of land

manufacturing
the process of making goods to sell

refuges
sheltered or protected places

settlers
people who moved to a new area

smugglers
people who illegally move things into or out of a country

Online Resources

To learn more about Rhode Island, visit our free resource websites below.

Visit **abdocorelibrary.com** or scan this QR code for free Common Core resources for teachers and students, including vetted activities, multimedia, and booklinks, for deeper subject comprehension.

Visit **abdobooklinks.com** or scan this QR code for free additional online weblinks for further learning. These links are routinely monitored and updated to provide the most current information available.

Learn More

Hansen, Grace. *Living through the Revolutionary War.* Abdo, 2024.

Kavon, Kana. *The 50 States.* DK, 2021.

Tieck, Sarah. *Rhode Island.* Abdo, 2020.

Index

About the Author

Janet Slingerland has authored more than two dozen nonfiction books on topics ranging from animals to Wi-Fi. She lives in New Jersey with her husband and three kids.